Nevada

by Jason Glaser

Consultant:
Dr. William Rowley
Department of History
University of Nevada, Reno

Capstone
press
Mankato, Minnesota

Capstone Press
151 Good Counsel Drive • P.O. Box 669 • Mankato, Minnesota 56002
http://www.capstone-press.com

Library of Congress Cataloging-in-Publication Data
Glaser, Jason.
   Nevada / by Jason Glaser.
   v. cm.—(Land of liberty)
   Includes bibliographical references (p. 61) and index.
   Contents: About Nevada—Land, climate, and wildlife—History of Nevada—
Government and politics—Economy and resources—People and culture—Nevada
cities—Nevada's land features—Chocolate nuggets—Nevada's flag and seal.
   ISBN 0-7368-2186-4 (hardcover)
   1. Nevada—Juvenile literature. [1. Nevada.] I. Title. II. Series.
F841.3.G58 2004
979.3—dc21   2002155468

Summary: An introduction to the geography, history, government, politics,
   economy, resources, people, and culture of Nevada, including maps, charts,
   and a recipe.

Editorial Credits

Christopher Harbo, editor; Jennifer Schonborn, series designer; Molly Nei, book
   designer; Enoch Peterson, illustrator; Kelly Garvin, photo researcher;
   Eric Kudalis, product planning editor

Photo Credits

Cover images: Red Rock Canyon, Houserstock/Dave G. Houser; Las Vegas skyline,
   Digital Vision

Bruce Coleman Inc./Bob & Clara Calhoun, 57; Bruce Coleman Inc./Mark Newman,
15; Capstone Press/Gary Sundermeyer, 54; Corbis/Bettmann, 26, 29; Corbis/Galen
Rowell, 40–41; Corbis/Lester Lefkowitz, 4; Corbis/Raymond Gehman, 17;
Corbis/Richard Cummins, 36; Courtesy of the U.S. Department of Energy, 34;
Cynthia A. Delaney/GeoIMAGERY, 46–47; Getty Images, 49; Getty Images/Hulton
Archive, 20, 23, 24–25, 27, 35, 58; Getty Images/Jeff Gross, 50; Houserstock/Dave
G. Houser, 38; Houserstock/Jan Butchofsky, 12–13; Houserstock/Steve Bly, 44; Jan
Wilson Jorolan/GeoIMAGERY, 43; John Alves/Mystic Wanderer Images, 39; Joseph
Franklin FitzGerald, 14; Kay Shaw, 30; Nevada State Library and Archives, 55
(bottom); One Mile Up Inc., 55 (top); Photo by Carol Diehl, 52; Steve Mulligan, 1,
18, 56, 63; Tom Till, 8; U.S. Postal Service, 59; Western Folklife Center, 53

Artistic Effects

Comstock, Corbis, PhotoDisc Inc.

1 2 3 4 5 6 08 07 06 05 04 03

Table of Contents

Hoover Dam holds back the waters of the Colorado River in Black Canyon.

Chapter 1

About Nevada

During the 1930s, nearly all of the people who lived in Boulder City, Nevada, had the same job. They were construction workers. The federal government built the town for workers building the Boulder Dam from 1932 to 1935. In 1947, President Harry S. Truman renamed the dam the Hoover Dam.

The Hoover Dam is one of the largest dams in the United States. It stands 726 feet (221 meters) tall. The dam is made from 3.25 million cubic yards (2.48 million cubic meters) of concrete. Hoover Dam stops and collects water from the Colorado River. The water forms Lake Mead, the largest artificial lake in the United States. The water flowing through

the dam's turbines generates enough electricity to serve 1.3 million people.

The Hoover Dam cost the United States $46 million to build. In the 1930s, every state in the United States sent workers and materials for the dam's construction.

The Silver State

Nevada is known as the Silver State. In the mid-1800s, settlers found silver and gold in Nevada. Many people moved to Nevada hoping to strike it rich in the mines.

Nevada is a large state with a small population. Nevada is the seventh largest state in area, but it has the 35th largest population. About two million people live there. More than half of them live in Las Vegas.

Nevada lies in the southwestern United States. California wraps around the western and southern borders. Oregon and Idaho make up the northern border of the state. Arizona and Utah lie along Nevada's eastern border.

Nevada Cities

OREGON

IDAHO

Legend

■	American Indian Reservation
★	Capital
●	City
⬭	Lake
○	Point of Interest
∿	River

Winnemucca ●

Elko ●

● Battle Mountain

NEVADA

UTAH

Sparks ■
● Reno
★ Carson City

Ely ●

Lake Tahoe

N
W — E
S

● Tonopah

Scale

Miles
0   40   80   120   160

0   40   80   120   160
Kilometers

Mesquite ●

Lake Mead

Las Vegas ●
Henderson ●●
Boulder City ○ Hoover Dam

ARIZONA

CALIFORNIA

Colorado River

PACIFIC OCEAN

Bristlecone pine trees grow at the base of Wheeler Peak in Nevada's Great Basin National Park.

Land, Climate, and Wildlife

Nevada's land lies high above sea level. Its highest point, Boundary Peak, is 13,140 feet (4,005 meters) above sea level. The state's lowest point at the Colorado River drops to 470 feet (143 meters) above sea level. Nevada's land can be divided into the Basin and Range region, the Columbia Plateau, and the Sierra Nevada region.

The Basin and Range Region

Most of Nevada lies in the Great Basin. This desert region covers about 200,000 square miles (518,000 square kilometers) of the western United States. The edges of the Great Basin are

higher than the center. Rivers and streams flow toward the middle of the basin. Most of the rivers and streams in the Great Basin flow into marshy areas. Some streams drain into low areas called sinks.

More than 150 mountain ranges cover Nevada's Basin and Range region. Most of these narrow ranges run from north to south. Smaller hills called buttes and low, flat mountains called mesas lie between the mountains. Grasslands and deserts surround many of the mountains in the region.

Many plants grow in the grasslands and deserts around Nevada's mountains. Fir, pine, alder, piñon pine, juniper, aspen, and other trees grow in the mountains. Cottonwood trees grow in lower areas along streams.

Some of the longest-living plants in the world grow in the Great Basin. The bristlecone pine can live nearly 5,000 years. The creosote bush can live up to 11,000 years.

Nevada's Basin and Range is home to many animals. Deer, antelope, black bear, longhorn sheep, and Rocky Mountain elk live in the higher areas. Reptiles, including tortoises,

Nevada's Land Features

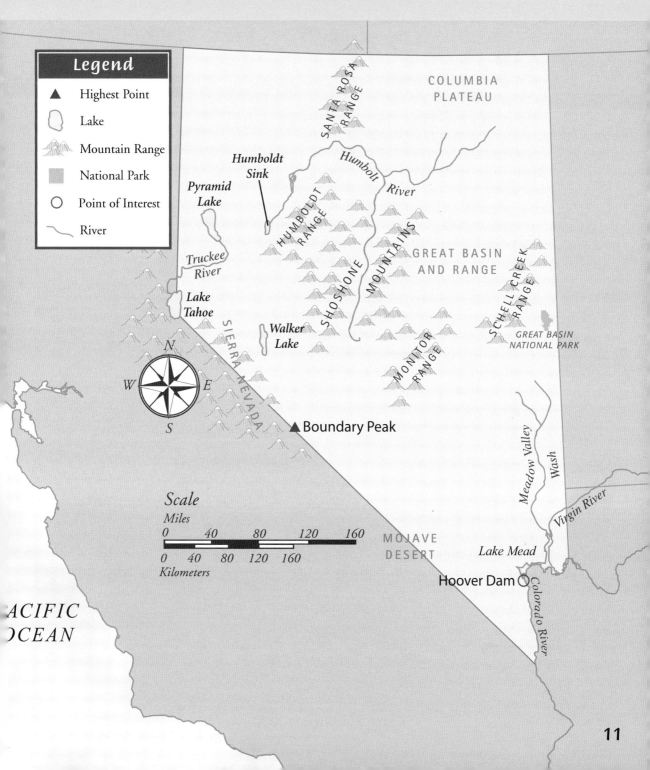

Legend

▲ Highest Point

Lake

Mountain Range

National Park

○ Point of Interest

River

COLUMBIA PLATEAU

SANTA ROSA RANGE

Humboldt Sink

Humbolt River

Pyramid Lake

HUMBOLDT RANGE

GREAT BASIN AND RANGE

SHOSHONE MOUNTAINS

SCHELL CREEK RANGE

Truckee River

Lake Tahoe

Walker Lake

GREAT BASIN NATIONAL PARK

N
W E
S

SIERRA NEVADA

MONITOR RANGE

▲ Boundary Peak

Meadow Valley Wash

Virgin River

Scale

Miles

0   40   80   120   160

0   40   80   120   160

Kilometers

MOJAVE DESERT

Lake Mead

Hoover Dam ○

Colorado River

PACIFIC OCEAN

sidewinder snakes, rattlesnakes, and Gila monsters also live in the Great Basin.

Columbia Plateau and Sierra Nevada

Northeastern Nevada lies in the Columbia Plateau. The few rivers in this area drain into Idaho's Snake River. The Snake River flows north into the Columbia River. The mountains in the Columbia Plateau are wider and flatter than the other

mountains in Nevada. Rabbits, coyotes, raccoons, and porcupines live in parts of the Columbia Plateau.

The tall mountains of the Sierra Nevada line the western border with California. The clear waters of Lake Tahoe cross the mountain border. Millions of people travel to Lake Tahoe each year. They enjoy fishing, biking, skiing, and other activities around the lake. East of Lake Tahoe, Reno, Sparks, and Carson City lie at the base of the Sierra Nevada.

Lake Tahoe's clear, blue waters are a popular place for people to jet ski and enjoy other outdoor activities.

Deserts and Wetlands

Part of the Mojave Desert extends from California into the southern tip of Nevada. The Mojave Desert is dry and the temperature varies. Temperatures can rise above 100 degrees Fahrenheit (38 degrees Celsius) during the day. At night, temperatures can fall to 40 degrees Fahrenheit (4 degrees Celsius). Plants and animals in the Mojave deal with great temperature changes.

Although much of Nevada is hot and dry, the state has a few wetland areas. About 12,000 years ago, lakes and seas

Pyramid Lake is located in the desert north of Reno. Explorer John Frémont named the lake for the large pyramid shaped rock that juts out of the water.

Wild Horses

More than half of the United States' wild horses live in Nevada. These horses are often smaller than domestic horses. Adults average about 5 feet (1.5 meters) tall from hoof to shoulder. Their hooves are hard and durable. Some wild horses have faint stripes like a zebra.

Both Nevada and the federal government have laws to protect wild horses. People are not allowed to capture or hunt them. In some places, farmers cannot use barbed wire fences. The fences could hurt traveling herds.

covering Nevada began to dry out. Today, small rivers and streams bring water to the state's lakes and wetlands. Walker Lake is an important stop for migrating loons and other water birds. Washoe Lake, Pyramid Lake, and other lakes in western Nevada provide food for geese, ducks, and pelicans. Frogs, toads, and salamanders also live in Nevada's wetlands.

Precipitation

Nevada receives less rain and snow than any other state. Most of Nevada receives only about 9 inches (23 centimeters) of rain per year. The mountain ranges around Nevada block most of the rain coming from the Pacific Ocean and the Gulf of Mexico.

Snow sometimes falls in northern Nevada and on the state's highest mountains. The Sierra Nevada area receives the most precipitation. These mountains receive about 25 inches (64 centimeters) of rain and snow per year.

Environmental Issues

Lack of water is the biggest danger to Nevada's environment. Long periods of dry weather can dry up small wetlands and streams, killing plants and animals.

Dry weather also increases the chances for wildfires. Fire can spread quickly in Nevada. Cheatgrass is spreading into the state. This grass burns easier than Nevada's other grasses. Brush fires quickly grow out of control.

The Derby Dam diverts water from the Truckee River to irrigate crops.
The river also is an important water source for Reno and Sparks.

Nevada also must be careful to prevent water pollution.
Small amounts of chemical waste from factories and mines
can hurt or kill the plants and animals. Nevada's wetlands
are home to many types of algae and insect life that cannot
be found anywhere else. Polluting the water could make
them extinct.

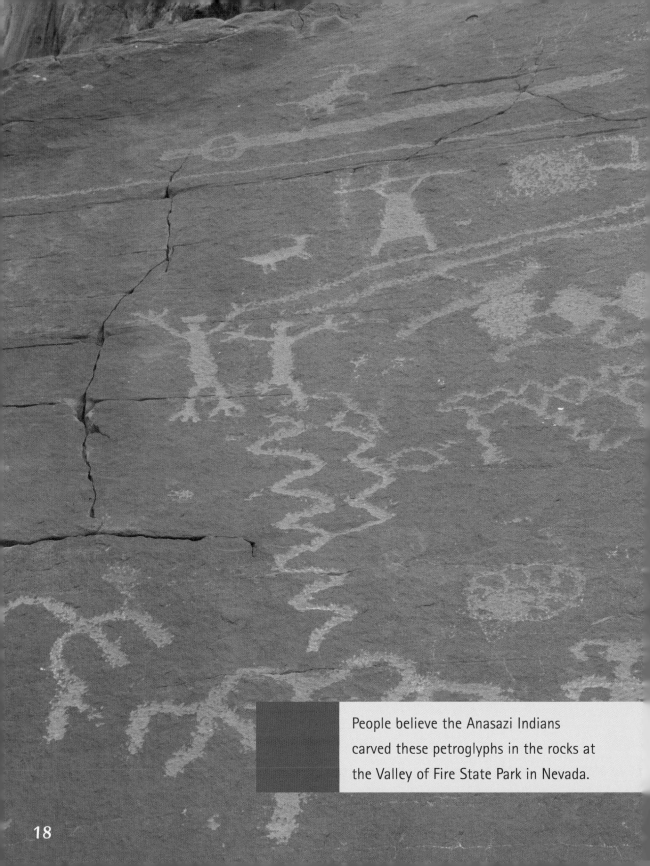

People believe the Anasazi Indians carved these petroglyphs in the rocks at the Valley of Fire State Park in Nevada.

Chapter 3

History of Nevada

Before European settlement, several native peoples lived in the Nevada area. The Basketmakers and the Anasazi were probably the first people to live in the area. Petroglyphs and pieces of baskets from these ancient people have been found in Nevada. These people left the Nevada area by A.D. 1250. When the first Europeans arrived in the late 1700s, the Shoshone, Paiute, and Washoe tribes lived in the Nevada area.

Spain was the first country to claim the land of Nevada. The first Spaniard to reach Nevada may have been Francisco Garcés. He was a missionary who traveled through Mexico's territory in 1776. Spain believed that it owned the land between its missions in California and the settlement of

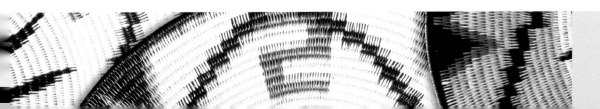

Santa Fe in New Mexico. In 1821, Mexico won independence from Spain. Mexico claimed areas of California, Nevada, Utah, Arizona, New Mexico, southern Colorado, and Texas.

After Mexico's independence, trappers and pioneers traveled into the Nevada area. They wanted to trap beavers. Canadian Peter Skene Ogden and American Jedediah Smith were two of the first trappers in Nevada. They explored the area in 1826.

In 1843, General John C. Frémont and Kit Carson explored much of Nevada for the United States. Frémont

In the 1840s, John C. Frémont explored areas in Nevada, California, and Oregon. He later became a major general for the Union army during the Civil War (1861–1865).

named many of the rivers and land features in the state. Frémont also made many maps of the area. These maps helped travelers pass through Nevada to reach California and Oregon.

By 1846, tensions over land had increased between Mexico and the United States. On May 13, 1846, the Mexican War (1846–1848) broke out between the two countries. The war ended when Mexico and the United States signed the Treaty of Guadalupe-Hidalgo. In the treaty, Mexico gave the United States a large area of land that included Nevada.

Settlers in Nevada

In 1847, Mormon leader Brigham Young brought his followers to the areas of Utah and Nevada. He was looking for a place where they could practice their religion freely. The Mormons settled in Salt Lake City, Utah. They called the large territory around their settlement the State of Deseret.

On September 9, 1850, U.S. President Millard Fillmore named the area the Utah Territory. A few days later, he named Young as the first acting governor of the Utah Territory.

Also in 1850, Mormon traders built a trading post in western Utah Territory along the California Trail.

"[Nevadans and sagebrush] are hardy and resilient, stubborn and independent, restrained by environment, and yet able to grow free."
—Robert Laxalt, Nevada writer and historian

Some Mormons settled in Carson County, which made up most of the future territory of Nevada. Mormon Station in Carson County was a popular trading post for travelers passing through Nevada.

Nevada Joins the Union

In 1856, James Buchanan was elected U.S. president. Buchanan wanted federal control over Mormon territories. Brigham Young did not believe the U.S. government should make laws for the Mormons. Young feared Buchanan would send soldiers to attack the Mormons. Young ordered all the Mormons in western Utah to return to Salt Lake City. After the Mormons were gone, settlers in the area began to govern themselves. They called the area the Nevada Territory.

In 1859, interest in creating a new U.S. territory grew when silver was discovered. A man named Henry Comstock spread news about the discovery of silver in the Nevada Territory. The silver mines became known as the Comstock

Advertisements for the Comstock Lode drew thousands of people to Virginia City in the 1860s.

Lode. President Buchanan realized the silver mines would bring more people into the area. In 1861, he signed a bill to separate the Nevada Territory from Utah.

Nevada's steps toward statehood began during the Civil War (1861–1865). In 1863, officials set up a convention to write a constitution for the territory. Nevada's voters did not approve the constitution. They did not agree with taxes on mining claims. In 1864, Nevada voters approved a second constitution. It allowed the state only limited taxes on the mines. Nevada became a state on October 31, 1864. Carson City became the capital. From 1861 to 1870, the state's population grew from 6,857 to 42,491.

Mining Woes

Miners in Nevada faced tough times in the late 1800s. During the Civil War, silver was used to make coins and luxury items.

Some soldiers were paid in silver coin. After the war, more silver was mined than the government needed. The price of silver began to fall. By the late 1870s, the national treasury stopped buying silver. Its price fell again. The Comstock mines ran out of silver ore and many mines closed. Many miners left Nevada.

As mines closed, ranching became more important to Nevada. Nevada's large open spaces provided room for livestock to roam. The new coast-to-coast railroad that crossed the state in 1869 helped ranchers ship cattle across

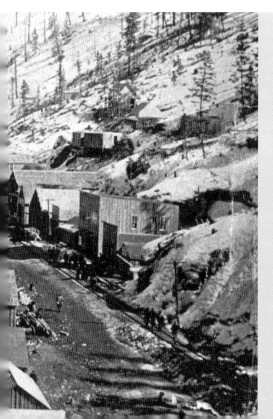

During the late 1800s, many silver mining camps were built at the base of the Sierra Nevada in western Nevada.

the country. Cattle ranching thrived for the next several years. Sheep grazing also became popular in Nevada.

Legalized Gambling

In the early 1900s, Nevada officials knew they needed to strengthen the state's economy. The state's ranches, and even new gold, silver, and copper mines, could not support the state's economy. In the 1930s, the Great Depression left many of the state's citizens without jobs. Nevada needed a solution.

Women gambled in Reno casinos in the mid-1930s.

Signs for clubs and casinos lined the busy streets of Las Vegas in the 1950s.

In 1931, Nevada legalized gambling in the state. Casinos became very popular. Casinos let customers bet on games. One popular game had people bet on which square of fabric a mouse would take a nap. Slot machines also became popular. Thousands of people from across the country traveled to cities like Reno and Las Vegas to gamble.

Did you know...?
In 1958, the Plowshare Program began at the Nevada Test Site. Plowshare tested the use of atomic energy for peaceful means. Thirty-five Plowshare blasts tested how well nuclear devices could move large amounts of dirt for digging canals and tunnels.

The casinos made a great deal of money. The money attracted the interest of mobsters. Bugsy Siegel and other famous mobsters started their own casinos and hotels. Others gave people money to start casinos so they could share in the profits. Mobsters made people afraid of going to Nevada. The FBI helped Nevada's police forces drive out the mob.

Recent Years

In the 1940s, silver again became an important part of Nevada's economy. People learned that silver could be used to make parts for electronic equipment. The United States needed these parts for equipment and weapons used during World War II (1939–1945).

In 1951, the U.S. government began using a site in southern Nevada to test nuclear weapons. More than 1,000 nuclear tests were done at the Nevada Test Site. While most of the tests took place underground, more than 100 bombs were tested above ground. The U.S. military tested how well homes, bunkers, and bridges could withstand nuclear blasts.

In the late 1900s, Nevada's population grew quickly. From 1990 to 2000, the population grew by 66 percent. Companies built new factories, airports, and hotels in the state.

Nevada's quick growth created new problems. The state needed new water sources for busy cities. Nevada also needed to protect water from pollution. In the 1990s, the state government worked to pass laws to protect the environment.

In 1951, soldiers trained during an atomic bomb test at the Nevada Test Site.

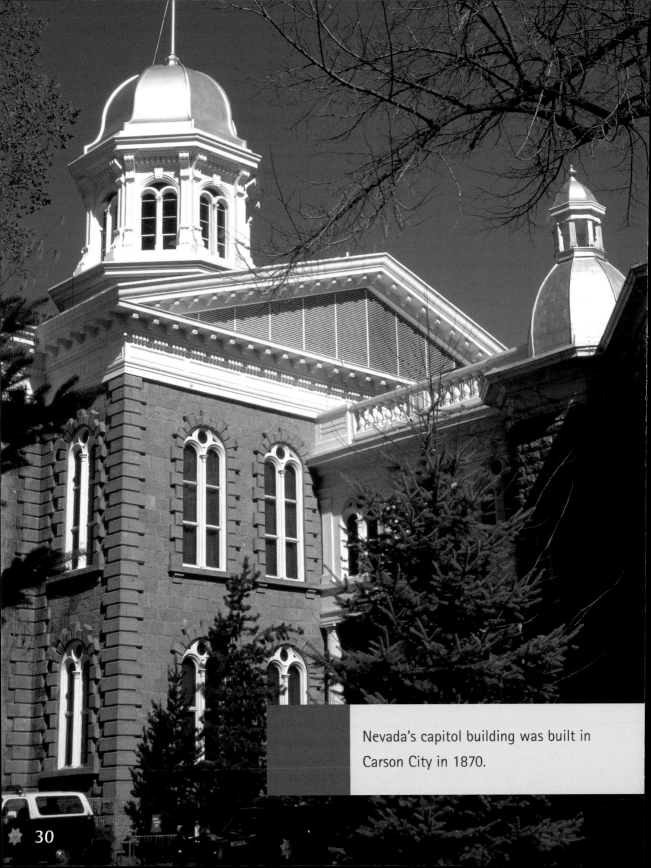

Nevada's capitol building was built in Carson City in 1870.

Chapter 4

Government and Politics

Nevada does not have much power in national politics. A small population gives the state only three representatives in the U.S. House of Representatives. Nevada has only five electoral votes out of the 538 in each presidential election. Presidential candidates receive all the electoral votes from states where they earn a majority of the popular vote.

Branches of Government

Nevada's government is divided into executive, legislative, and judicial branches. The executive branch enforces state laws and creates the state budget. The governor, the lieutenant

governor, and the attorney general are the top members of the executive branch. Since 1996, all elected executive officials are limited to two terms.

The legislative branch is divided into the state senate and an assembly. The legislature writes and changes state laws. Nevada has 21 state senators and 42 state assembly members. Senate members are elected to four-year terms. Assembly members are elected to two-year terms. Both senators and assembly members can serve only 12 years. The legislature meets from February to June each odd-numbered year.

The Nevada Supreme Court leads Nevada's judicial branch. Seven justices serve on the supreme court. The most experienced justice serves as Chief Justice. Below the supreme court, Nevada has district courts in nine judicial districts. District courts hear the state's largest cases. They also hear cases appealed from the state's justice and municipal courts. Justice and municipal courts hear cases dealing with local laws.

Nevada's State Government

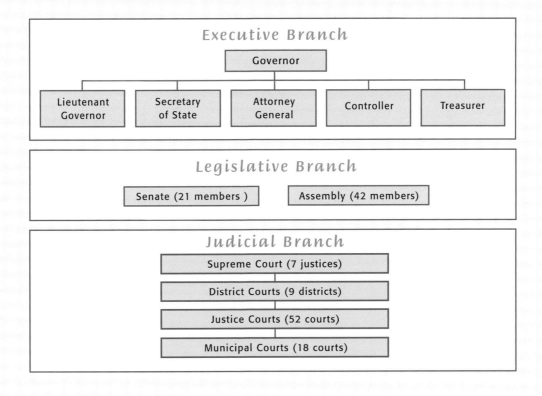

Executive Branch

Governor

Lieutenant Governor | Secretary of State | Attorney General | Controller | Treasurer

Legislative Branch

Senate (21 members) | Assembly (42 members)

Judicial Branch

Supreme Court (7 justices)

District Courts (9 districts)

Justice Courts (52 courts)

Municipal Courts (18 courts)

Nevada Land Issues

The use of land by the federal government is an important
issue in Nevada. Over the years, Nevada has fought for greater
control over federal land in the state. The U.S. government
owns more than 86 percent of the land in Nevada. Some land

is used for national forests and Great Basin National Park. Other areas have been used for nuclear weapons testing.

Since the 1980s, the U.S. government has been studying Nevada's Yucca Mountain. The government wants to store nuclear waste under the mountain. In 2002, Nevada Governor Kenny Guinn protested the presidential decision to use the mountain to store nuclear waste. His veto did not change the president's decision, but it showed that Nevadans did not want nuclear waste stored in their state.

The U.S. government has considered storing nuclear waste under Yucca Mountain since the 1980s. Yucca Mountain is located about 100 miles (161 kilometers) northwest of Las Vegas.

Pat Nixon

Former First Lady Pat Nixon grew up in Nevada. Born Thelma "Pat" Catherine Ryan in 1912, Pat grew up in Ely, Nevada. She went to the University of Southern California in the 1930s. There she met Richard Nixon. Pat and Richard married in 1940. In 1968, Richard was elected president.

As First Lady, Pat traveled the world as an ambassador of the United States. In 1969, she traveled to Vietnam. She became the first First Lady to visit a combat zone. In 1970, she helped send supplies to Peru after the country suffered an earthquake. The Peruvian government awarded Pat the Grand Cross of the Order of the Sun. She was the first woman to receive this award.

Pat believed that the White House should be open to everyone. She hired guides to give tours to people who could not see or hear. She held tours at night for people who worked during the day. She invited thousands to go to church services on Sundays in the East Room.

Pat died June 22, 1993. She is buried at the Nixon Library in California.

The Colorado Bell Hotel and Casino in Laughlin, Nevada, looks like a giant Mississippi River paddle wheel riverboat.

Chapter 5

Economy and Resources

Tourism, mining, manufacturing, and agriculture all support Nevada's economy. These industries make enough money yearly to give Nevada one of the most stable economies in the United States. Almost all of Nevada's income comes from these businesses. Nevada does not have state income taxes, corporate taxes, or business franchise taxes.

Tourism and Entertainment

The tourism industry is Nevada's largest source of income. Over 40 million people visit the state each year. Many tourists come to gamble at casinos in Reno and Las Vegas.

Stratosphere Tower

The Stratosphere Tower in Las Vegas is the tallest building west of the Mississippi River. It stands 1,149 feet (350 meters) tall. People can see all of Las Vegas from the observation deck. The world's highest roller coaster, the High Roller, runs around the Stratosphere. It thrills riders 909 feet (277 meters) above the ground.

Nevada taxes the money that casinos make from gamblers. The state receives more than $700 million in taxes from casinos each year.

Nevada has many scenic places to visit. In western Nevada, tourists golf, hike, bicycle, and fish in the Lake Tahoe area. In eastern Nevada, thousands of people tour Hoover Dam and hike in Great Basin National Park.

More than 450,000 people work in Nevada's service industry. Many work at casinos. Thousands more work at hotels throughout the state. Many restaurants and shops for tourists employ workers. Some people even work as tour guides in old mining ghost towns.

Agriculture

Livestock is Nevada's main agricultural product. Some of Nevada's valleys have enough grass to support sheep and cattle. Ranchers also irrigate fields to grow grass so cattle can graze. Although most livestock is sold for meat, some Nevada farmers keep dairy cattle to produce milk.

Nevada ranchers use horses to herd cattle on their large ranches.

Nevada farmers also grow a wide variety of crops. Potatoes, garlic, wheat, and onions are among Nevada's food crops. Farmers also grow cotton, Christmas trees, alfalfa, and oats in the state.

Mining

Mining in Nevada continues to be important. Nevada mines produce gold, silver, salt, silicate, limestone, copper and lithium.

About 10,000 workers in Nevada mine gold and silver. Miners dig for gold in the northern part of the state. Nevada supplies about three-fourths of the gold used in the United States. Nevada's mines are the third largest source of gold in the world. In 2000, Nevada mined more than 8 million ounces (227 million grams) of gold. It was worth more than $2.4 billion.

Miners dig for silver in southern Nevada. Nevada is the top producer of silver in the United States. The state's silver

The Manhattan Mine is an open pit gold mine in central Nevada. The state's gold mines produce 10 percent of the world's gold.

mines supply about 30 percent of the nation's silver and 3 percent of the world's silver. Silver production was worth $116 million in 2000.

Manufacturing

Manufacturing provides some of the state's revenue. General Motors operates an auto parts plant in Sparks. Several companies make stone, clay, and glass products from the minerals in Nevada. Nevada also supplies the country with large amounts of concrete, machinery, and printed paper materials.

Other Industries

The federal government is a large employer in the state. Thousands of military personnel work at military bases and other government facilities in the state. The government also employs people at hospitals, schools, offices, and restaurants in those places.

Nevada also has some energy resources. Oil wells lie in the eastern part of the state. Most electricity is generated at

The Hoover Dam uses 17 turbines to generate electricity. Nevada, Arizona, and California all use electricity from Hoover Dam.

hydroelectric plants on dams along the Colorado River. These plants use the energy created by falling water to make electricity. The electricity is supplied to areas in southern Nevada, Arizona, and California. Coal-burning power plants produce electricity for larger cities. Some power plants use steam produced underground to make electricity.

Hotels and casinos light up the night on the Las Vegas Strip.

Chapter 6

People and Culture

Nevada has the highest growth rate in the United States. Its population is growing because people are drawn to the state's jobs and businesses. Most of these jobs are around the big cities. Highways and public transportation allow cities to expand. The suburbs of larger cities have grown very quickly. In 1985, less than 100 people lived in Laughlin, near Las Vegas. By 2002, more than 12,000 people lived there.

As the large cities grow, many rural areas are becoming less populated. Some small towns in central Nevada are struggling to survive. People are not moving to these towns. Most small towns do not have large businesses that provide jobs.

American Indians

The American Indians living in Nevada are working to keep their culture alive. The Washoe are famous for their baskets. Over time, fewer people have been taught how to weave baskets. The Washoe, Paiute, and Shoshone have all tried to pass on art forms, stories, and traditions to their children. Some tribes have also started programs to teach members how to speak their native languages.

The Basque

Between 4,000 and 5,000 people of Basque heritage live in Nevada. The Basque people come from a small area in Europe called Euskal Herria. Euskal Herria is near France and Spain. The Basque, or Euskaldunak, people have a unique language called Euskara.

During the early 1800s, many Basques immigrated to Latin America. They became farmers and sheepherders. When

People run, jump, and climb to avoid charging bulls during the "Running from the Bulls" event at the National Basque Festival in Elko, Nevada.

Nevada's Ethnic Backgrounds

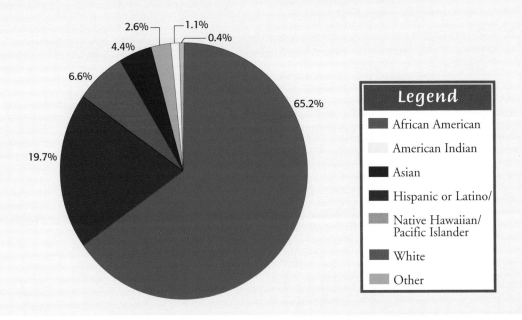

gold and silver were discovered in the United States, some Basques traveled to California and Nevada. Although few found gold, excellent sheepherding skills allowed the Basque to make a living by ranching.

Basque communities continue to be proud of their heritage. Elko holds a Basque festival every year. The University of Nevada, Reno, has a Center for Basque Studies. It teaches people about the Euskara language, Basque culture, and Basque history.

The Entertainment State

For many people, entertainment comes to mind when they think of Nevada. Nevada holds some of the largest shows, concerts, and performances in the country. Some entertainers perform most of their shows in Las Vegas instead of touring. Singers Celine Dion, Sammy Davis Jr., and Frank Sinatra created shows that were performed only in Las Vegas. Magicians Siegfried and Roy are famous for using white tigers during their Las Vegas performances.

Siegfried and Roy have amazed Las Vegas audiences with their magic for more than 30 years.

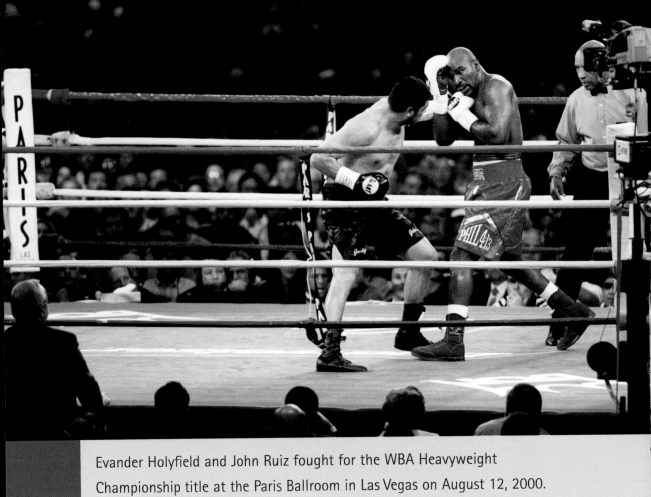

Evander Holyfield and John Ruiz fought for the WBA Heavyweight
Championship title at the Paris Ballroom in Las Vegas on August 12, 2000.

Nevada does not have any professional sports teams.
Nevada holds special sporting events instead. In Las Vegas,
boxing and professional wrestling matches take place several
times throughout the year. Professional rodeos also take place
in Nevada. Some of Nevada's golf courses hold PGA and
LPGA tournaments.

"I may not know much about a white-faced steer, but I know people. That is my business. And I must say I'm in love with the folks in Nevada."
—Bing Crosby, entertainer and honorary mayor of Elko, Nevada, from 1948 to 1977

Nevada on Film

In the 1920s, filmmakers from California needed open areas to shoot movies. They felt most of the areas in California had been used too many times. Warm temperatures, large areas of land, and few people made Nevada an attractive location to make movies.

More than 500 movies have been filmed in Nevada. The state's rugged landscape and large cities have been perfect for many movies. John Wayne filmed several westerns in Nevada. Pyramid Lake north of Reno was used as the Dead Sea for the movie *The Greatest Story Ever Told*. Reno and Las Vegas have also been colorful settings for movies. *Viva Las Vegas, Rain Man*, *Austin Powers*, and *Ocean's 11* have all used Nevada's casinos to tell their stories.

Modern Cowboys

Nevada's people are proud of their western folk stories and culture. In 1980, a man named Hal Cannon created the

Extraterrestrial Highway

In 1996, Governor Bob Miller rededicated State Highway 375 as "Extraterrestrial Highway." The highway runs by a top-secret Air Force base called Area 51.

People have reported sightings of unidentified flying objects (UFOs) near Area 51. Some people believe these UFOs are alien spaceships. Others think these sightings are military aircraft.

The Extraterrestrial Highway attracts "alien hunting" tourists. Billboards along the highway encourage any visiting aliens to land in the area.

Western Folklife Center in Elko. Cannon collected stories, letters, pictures, and artwork from people who had settled in the west.

Visitors to the Western Folklife Center can read cowboy poetry. Cowboy poets wrote poems during trail drives. A ballad was one kind of cowboy poem that was popular in the

1870s and 1880s. It rhymed and often told about cowboy life. In 1985, the Western Folklife Center held a Cowboy Poetry Gathering. It was so successful that one has been held every year since then. The Cowboy Poetry Gathering runs for nine days every January in Elko.

Silver mines, casinos, and cowboys are the backdrop for Nevada's rich history and culture. Lake Tahoe's blue waters, Las Vegas' bright lights, and Hoover Dam's grand size keep people coming back to the Silver State year after year.

Women and men read poetry at the Cowboy Poetry Gathering in Elko each January.

Chocolate Nuggets

Chocolate nuggets were a favorite recipe of former Nevada governor Bob Miller. These milk chocolate candies are quick and easy to make.

Ingredients

1 egg
12 ounces (340 grams)
    milk chocolate chips
½ teaspoon (2.5 mL) vanilla
dash of salt
¼ cup (60 mL) milk

Equipment

microwave-safe bowl
liquid measuring cup
measuring spoons
wire whisk
spoon
blender
spatula
miniature dessert cups

What You Do

1. Crack the egg into a microwave-safe bowl and beat lightly with a wire whisk.

2. Add chocolate chips, vanilla, salt, and milk to the bowl.

3. Stir ingredients with a spoon until all of the chocolate chips are coated with egg.

4. Put the bowl in the microwave. Heat on high for 2 minutes.

5. Pour mixture into a blender. Use a spatula to scrape extra chocolate in the bowl into the blender.

6. Blend mixture for 1 minute.

7. Pour the blended mixture into miniature dessert cups.

8. Refrigerate dessert cups 6 hours or until they are set.

Makes 12 nuggets

Nevada's Flag and Seal

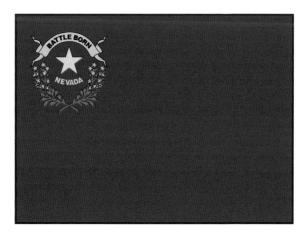

Nevada's Flag

Nevada's flag has changed several times since the first flag was adopted in 1905. Today, Nevada's flag is dark blue. In the flag's upper left corner, the words "Battle Born" are on a gold ribbon. These words reflect Nevada's statehood during the Civil War. A silver star, the state's name, and a wreath of sagebrush are below the ribbon. The silver star represents Nevada's silver mines. Sagebrush is the state flower.

Nevada's State Seal

The importance of agriculture, mining, transportation, and communication are reflected in Nevada's state seal. A bundle of wheat, a sickle, and a plow represent agriculture. A miner pulling a load of ore with his team of horses stands for the state's mining history. A train and a line of telegraph poles at the base of the mountains represent transportation and communication.

Almanac

Nickname: The Silver State

Population: 1,998,257 (U.S. Census 2000)
Population rank: 35th

Capital: Carson City

Largest cities: Las Vegas, Henderson, Reno, North Las Vegas, Sparks

Agriculture

Agricultural products: Cattle, hay, dairy products, potatoes

Climate

Average summer temperature: 69 degrees Fahrenheit (21 degrees Celsius)

Average winter temperature: 31 degrees Fahrenheit (minus 0.5 degree Celsius)

Average annual precipitation: 9 inches (23 centimeters)

Area: 110,567 square miles (286,369 square kilometers)
Size rank: 7th

Highest point: Boundary Peak, 13,140 feet (4,005 meters) above sea level

Lowest Point: Colorado River, 470 feet (143 meters) above sea level

Geography

Bristlecone pine

56

Mountain bluebird

Bird: Mountain bluebird

Fish: Lahontan cutthroat trout

Flower: Sagebrush

Grass: Indian ricegrass

Economy

Natural resources: Silver, gold, copper, salt, silicate, limestone, lithium, wood

Types of industry: Tourism, mining, machinery, printing and publishing, food processing, electrical equipment

Symbols

Metal: Silver

Reptile: Desert tortoise

Rock: Sandstone

Song: "Home Means Nevada," by Bertha Raffetto

Trees: Single leaf piñon and bristlecone pine

Government

First governor: Henry G. Blasdel, 1864–1870

Statehood: October 31, 1864 (36th state)

U.S. Representatives: 3

U.S. Senators: 2

U.S. electoral votes: 5

Counties: 17

Timeline

State History

1776
Francisco Garcés travels through Mexico and Nevada.

1843
John Frémont leads an expedition into Nevada.

1850
Mormon traders settle in Western Utah Territory.

1859
Silver discovered in the Nevada area.

1861
United States creates the Nevada Territory.

1864
Nevada becomes a state.

U.S. History

1620
Pilgrims establish Massachusetts Bay Colony.

1775–1783
American colonies fight for independence from Great Britain in the Revolutionary War.

1812–1814
The United States fights Great Britain in the War of 1812.

1846–1848
The United States fights Mexico in the Mexican War.

1861–1865
Union states fight Confederate states in the Civil War.

1935
Hoover Dam is completed.

1951
The U.S. government begins testing atomic bombs in Nevada.

2002
The U.S. government decides to store more than 77,000 tons of nuclear waste under Yucca Mountain. Governor Guinn symbolically vetoes the proposal.

1931
Nevada legalizes gambling.

1929–1939
The United States experiences the Great Depression.

1964
U.S. Congress passes the Civil Rights Act, which makes discrimination illegal.

1914–1918
World War I is fought; the United States enters the war in 1917.

1939–1945
World War II is fought; the United States enters the war in 1941.

2001
Terrorists attack the Pentagon and the World Trade Center on September 11.

Words to Know

casino (kuh-SEE-noh)—a place where adults gamble

domestic (duh-MESS-tik)—no longer wild; people keep domestic animals as pets or raise them for food.

gamble (GAM-buhl)—to bet money on the outcome of a game or event

hydroelectric (hye-droh-i-LEK-trik)—to do with the production of electricity from moving water

irrigation (ihr-uh-GAY-shuhn)—supplying water to crops using channels or pipes

lode (LOHD)—a rich supply of ore in the ground

mission (MISH-uhn)—a church or place that is built to teach people about Christian religions

mobster (MOB-stur)—a member of a criminal gang

Mormon (MOR-muhn)—a member of The Church of Jesus Christ of Latter-day Saints

rodeo (ROH-dee-oh)—a competition where people rope cattle and ride horses and bulls

sink (SINK)—an area of low land that collects water

territory (TERR-uh-tor-ee)—land under control of a country

To Learn More

DuTemple, Lesley A. *The Hoover Dam.* Great Building Feats. Minneapolis: Lerner Publications, 2003.

Hopkins, Ellen. *Tarnished Legacy: The Story of the Comstock Lode.* Cover to Cover Books. Logan, Iowa: Perfection Learning, 2001.

Stefoff, Rebecca. *Nevada.* Celebrate the States. New York: Benchmark Books, 2001.

Stein, R. Conrad. *Nevada.* America the Beautiful. New York: Children's Press, 2000.

Internet Sites

Do you want to find out more about Nevada?
Let FactHound, our fact-finding hound dog, do the research for you.

Here's how:
1) Visit ***http://www.facthound.com***
2) Type in the **Book ID** number:
   0736821864
3) Click on **FETCH IT**.

FactHound will fetch Internet sites picked by our editors just for you!

Places to Write and Visit

Buckaroo Hall of Fame
30 West Winnemucca Boulevard
Winnemucca, NV 89445

Lied Discovery Children's Museum
833 Las Vegas Boulevard North
Las Vegas, NV 89101

Nevada Commission on Tourism
401 North Carson Street
Carson City, NV 89701

Nevada Historical Society
1650 North Virginia Street
Reno, NV 89503

Western Folklife Center
501 Railroad Street
Elko, NV 89801

Hundreds of shoes hang from the "Shoe Tree" near U.S. Highway 50 in Nevada. Legend says a young woman started the tradition by throwing her shoes in the tree when she became angry with her husband.

Index